MARCO POLO

—Other titles in the **Great Explorers of the World** series—

COLUMBUS
Opening Up
the New World

ISBN-13: 978-1-59845-101-6
ISBN-10:   1-59845-101-4

LA SALLE
French Explorer
of the Mississippi

ISBN-13: 978-1-59845-098-9
ISBN-10:   1-59845-098-0

HENRY HUDSON
Discoverer of the Hudson River

ISBN-13: 978-1-59845-123-8
ISBN-10:   1-59845-123-5

MAGELLAN
First to Circle the Globe

ISBN-13: 978-1-59845-097-2
ISBN-10:   1-59845-097-2

HERNANDO DE SOTO
Spanish Conquistador
in the Americas

ISBN-13: 978-1-59845-104-7
ISBN-10:   1-59845-104-9

VASCO DA GAMA
Discovering the
Sea Route to India

ISBN-13: 978-1-59845-127-6
ISBN-10:   1-59845-127-8

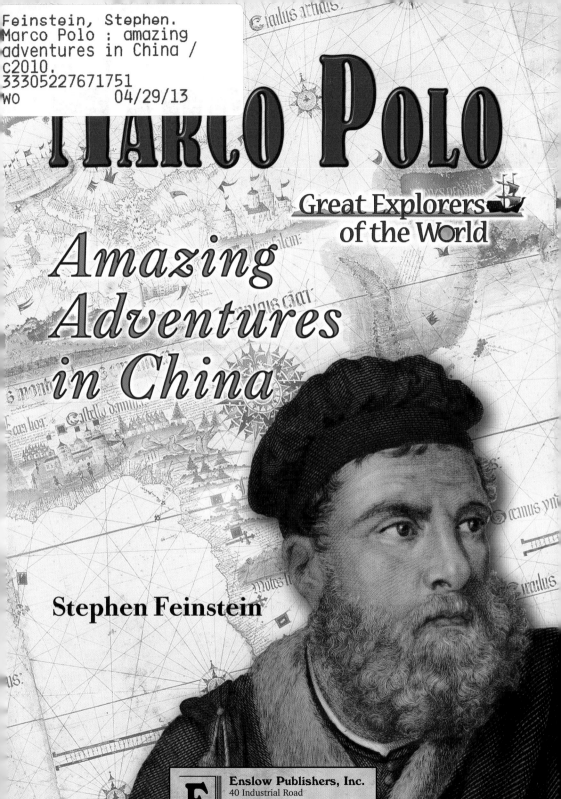

MARCO POLO

Great Explorers
of the World

Amazing
Adventures
in China

Stephen Feinstein

Enslow Publishers, Inc.
40 Industrial Road
Box 398
Berkeley Heights, NJ 07922
USA
http://www.enslow.com

Library of Congress Cataloging-in-Publication Data

Feinstein, Stephen.
  Marco Polo : amazing adventures in China / Stephen Feinstein.
      p. cm. — (Great explorers of the world)
  Includes bibliographical references and index.
  Summary: "Examines the life of Italian explorer Marco Polo, including a childhood
in Venice, his travels in China and the Mongol empire, his service to Kublai Khan,
and his imprisonment in Genoa"—Provided by publisher.
  ISBN-13: 978-1-59845-103-0
  ISBN-10: 1-59845-103-0
  1. Polo, Marco, 1254-1323?—Juvenile literature. 2. Explorers—Italy—
Biography—Juvenile literature. 3. Voyages and travels—Juvenile
literature. 4. Travel, Medieval—Juvenile literature. 5. China—
Description and travel—Juvenile literature. 6. Polo, Marco, 1254–
1323?—Imprisonment—Juvenile literature. I. Title.
  G370.P9F45 2010
  915.104'24—dc22
                              2008040344

Printed in the United States of America
012012 Lake Book Manufacturing, Inc., Melrose Park, IL
10 9 8 7 6 5 4 3 2

To Our Readers: We have done our best to make sure all Internet Addresses in this book were
active and appropriate when we went to press. However, the author and the publisher have no control over and assume no liability for the material available on those Internet sites or on other Web
sites they may link to. Any comments or suggestions can be sent by e-mail to comments@enslow.com
or to the address on the back cover.

♻ Enslow Publishers, Inc., is committed to printing our books on recycled paper. The paper in every
book contains 10% to 30% post-consumer waste (PCW). The cover board on the outside of each book
contains 100% PCW. Our goal is to do our part to help young people and the environment too!

Illustration Credits: Bibliotheque Nationale, Paris © World History / Topham / The Image
Works, pp. 28–29, 36; From *The Book of Ser Marco Polo*, Yule-Cordier Edition, pp. 78, 94; Enslow
Publishers, Inc., pp. 58–59; The Granger Collection, New York, pp. 3, 11, 14, 46–47, 54–55, 70–71,
86–87, 98; © iStockphoto / Robert Churchill, p. 75; © Jupiterimages Corporation, pp. 24–25, 65;
Public domain image, Wikipedia, p. 101; © Shutterstock®, pp. 22, 57; Werner Forman Archive /
Barder Institute of Fine Arts, Birmingham. Location: 15. © 2004 Werner Forman / TopFoto / The
Image Works, p. 92; Werner Forman Archive / San Marco Treasury, Venice. Location: 08. © Werner
Forman Archive / Topham / The Image Works, p. 90.

Compass Illustration Used in Chapter Openers: © Shutterstock®.

Cover Illustration: The Granger Collection, New York (Portrait of Marco Polo).

Contents

Explorer Timeline

1167 — Birth of Genghis Khan, Mongol leader.

1204 — Venetians and European allies sack Constantinople.

1210 — Genghis Khan invades China.

1215 — Birth of Kublai Khan.

1220 — Mongols conquer Persian Empire.

1227 — Death of Genghis Khan.

1234 — Mongols take control of northern China.

1241 — Victory of Mongols over European knights in Poland; Mongols threaten western Europe.

1253 — Niccolò and Maffeo Polo set sail from Venice to Constantinople.

1254 — Marco Polo, the son of Niccolò Polo, is born in Venice on September 15.

1258 — Mongols capture Baghdad.

1260 — Kublai Khan becomes the Great Khan of the Mongols, ruler of the Mongol Empire; Niccolò and Maffeo Polo travel to Cathay (China).

1262 — Niccolò and Maffeo Polo are caught in a war between two rival Mongol lords; they seek refuge at Bukhara, where they receive an invitation to Cathay to meet Kublai Khan.

1266 — The Polo brothers arrive at the court of Kublai Khan in Khanbalik (present-day Beijing), China.

1269 — Niccolò and Maffeo return to Venice; Niccolò's wife has died leaving a son, Marco.

1271 — Niccolò, Maffeo, and Marco leave Venice for China.

1274 — The Polos reach China.

1275— The three Polos reach Kublai Khan's summer palace at Xanadu.

1275 — Marco travels throughout the Mongol Empire
−1292 in the service of Kublai Khan.

1291— Kublai Khan sends the Polos to escort a
−1294 Mongol princess to her betrothed in the Ilkhanate in Persia. The Polos travel by sea from the Chinese port city of Quanzhou, Sri Lanka, India, and finally to Persia.

1292— The Polos and Princess Kokachin sail from Cathay for Persia.

1294— Kublai Khan dies.

1295— The Polos return to Venice after a twenty-four-year absence.

1298— Marco is captured and imprisoned in Genoa. During his imprisonment, he dictates the story of his travels in Asia to a fellow prisoner, Rustichello of Pisa. The book (known alternately as *Il Milione, The Description of the World* or *The Travels of Marco Polo*) becomes a huge success in Europe.

1299— Marco Polo is released from prison, marries, and has three children. He never leaves Venice again.

1324— Marco Polo dies at home at age seventy on January 9.

Chapter 1

Danger in the Desert

In the year 1271, Niccolò and Maffeo Polo set out from Venice on a long and dangerous journey to visit Kublai Khan in far off Cathay (present-day China). This was their second journey to Cathay. This time, Niccolò's seventeen-year-old son Marco accompanied the Venetian merchants.

On their previous trip, the Polo brothers had been greatly impressed with the riches of the East—the exotic spices, silks, and jewels. They hoped that their trading activities this time would bring them great wealth. It would take the Polos four years to reach their destination.

THE DREADED KARAUNAS

In 1272, after traveling for a year, the three Polos had come as far as Persia (present-day Iran). They now had to cross the Dasht-e-Lut, the Desert of Emptiness, in eastern Persia. Beyond the desert lay the Persian Gulf. At the bustling port of Hormuz, the Polos planned to find a ship that would carry them eastward across the sea to India. From there, they hoped to sail to the coast of distant Cathay.

The Polos had been warned about a desert tribe called the Karaunas that preyed upon travelers. The Polos believed that there was safety in numbers. So they traded their horses for camels and joined a large caravan of merchants traveling across the desert. According to Marco Polo, the Karaunas were from Tartar and Indian ancestry.

In his book *The Travels*, Marco Polo wrote that Nigudar, the powerful king of the Karaunas, "took his 10,000 followers, a villainous band of cutthroats,"[1] and captured the city of Lahore (in present-day Pakistan). According to Marco, Nigudar remained there as ruler. He and his followers made war on the other Tartars who lived near his kingdom. (The "Tartars" may actually have been Mongols. In his book, Marco Polo refers to Mongols as "Tartars." But the Tartars were just one of the tribes belonging to the Mongol Empire.)

Marco Polo described the strategy of Nigudar and his raiders:

> In their marauding expeditions, which may extend to thirty or forty days' journey, they usually ride towards Rudbar [near the southern part of the Desert of Emptiness]. This is because in the winter all the merchants who come to do business in Hormuz, while they are awaiting the arrival of the merchants from India, send their mules and camels, which have grown thin from the long journey, to the plain of Rudbar to fatten on the rich pasturage; and here the Karaunas are on the look out to seize them.[2]

Marco Polo, dressed in Tartar attire, had much to worry about on his journey to China.

"Magic Fog"

According to Marco Polo, the Karaunas had the power of raising a magic fog when they raided. While the choking dust frightened their victims, the Karaunas attacked. Historians explain the magic fog as dry fog, fine dust particles frequently stirred up by the hot desert winds. While the Karaunas did not truly possess magic powers, they were nevertheless ruthless bandits, robbing and often killing those of their victims who were unable to escape.

The Karaunas' fearsome reputation caused desert travelers to turn pale at the very mention of their name. Marco Polo apparently believed in the magic powers of the Karaunas. He wrote:

> These robbers, when they are bent on raiding and pillage, work an enchantment by diabolic art so that the day turns dark and no one can see more than a very short distance. This darkness they spread over an extent of seven days' journey. They know the country very well. When they have brought on the darkness, they ride side by side, sometimes as many as 10,000 of them together, sometimes more, sometimes less, so that they over-spread all the region they mean to rob. Nothing they find in the open country, neither man nor beast nor goods, can escape capture. When they have taken captives who cannot pay a ransom, they kill all the old, and the young they lead away and sell them as bondsmen and slaves.[3]

The Karaunas, of course, did not raise a magic fog. They earned their reputation by waiting to attack a caravan until a sandstorm would arise. Strong desert winds would blow thick clouds of dust across the vast landscape, obscuring everything in sight.

A NARROW ESCAPE

As the Polos traveled across the desert, at some point the air began to fill with dust. The caravan became enveloped in a dry fog. This was the moment the Karaunas had been waiting for. Writer Richard Humble describes what must have occurred:

> We can see the Polos' caravan winding across the Rudbar plain, and imagine the growing discomfort and uneasiness of the men in the column as the heat grew ever more unbearable and the dust-haze deepened, rising and reddining the sun to a dim copper blur. Then, out of the gloom, the sudden, unnerving attack. The column, doubtless already badly put out of joint by the descent of the dust-fog, broke in panic. Fast and instant flight was the only chance of survival, and this was just what the three Polos took.[4]

The Polos realized that their survival depended on their ability to outrun the Karaunas. They took off as fast as their camels could run. As the Polos emerged from the thickest part of the fog, the Karaunas saw them and took off after them at a

Marco, Maffeo, and Niccolò Polo narrowly escaped the Karaunas. The traveling merchants often traded in the towns they stopped in along the way.

full gallop. As the chase continued across the plain, the hunters closed in on their prey. But fortunately for the Polos, the town of Kamasal soon appeared before them.

As Marco Polo noted in his book, "There are many towns and villages with earthen walls of great height and thickness to protect them."[5] Not a moment too soon, the three Polos entered Kamasal. As the town's gates closed behind them, the Polos must have breathed a sigh of relief. The Karaunas turned back, probably to plunder whatever remained of the caravan.

Safe inside Kamasal, the Polos would wait to join the next caravan to continue across the Rudbar plain toward Hormuz. In describing the event that had transpired, Marco wrote, "I assure you that Messer [Master] Marco himself narrowly evaded capture by these robbers in the darkness they had made. He escaped to a town called Kamasal; but many of his companions were taken captive and sold, and some put to death."[6]

"Thus," wrote Marco, "I have recounted the matter to you just as it occurred. And now we shall go on to tell you of other things."[7]

Chapter 2

TWO MERCHANTS OF VENICE

Marco

Polo was born in Venice on September 15, 1254. Venice is a city in present-day Italy. But in the thirteenth century, the country of Italy did not yet exist. The area that would one day become Italy consisted of various kingdoms and city-states. By the mid-thirteenth century, Venice had become one of the most important centers of trade in medieval Europe. It served as the gateway to the riches of the East.

Marco's father Niccolò and his uncle Maffeo were successful Venetian merchants who would become known for their travels in Asia. The Polo brothers were not the first merchants to travel from Venice to Asia. But they would share in Marco's fame after he wrote his book about their travels.

THE REPUBLIC OF VENICE: "LA SERENISSIMA"

The city-state of Venice, known as La Serenissima (the most serene), was unique for its beauty, power, and wealth. A few years before Marco Polo's birth, an Italian named Boncompagno da Signa had written of Venice as "incomparable . . . its floor is the sea, its roof is the sky, and its walls are the flow of its waters; this singular city takes away the power of speech because you cannot nor will ever be able to find a realm such as this."[1]

Overland travel in thirteenth-century Europe was slow and dangerous, something to be avoided if at all possible. A journey by horse-drawn cart from Venice to Paris took about five weeks. Most Europeans feared the unknown and therefore did not travel. But Venetians were different. Situated on a lagoon at the northern end of the Adriatic Sea, Venice was a bustling seaport. Many people in Venice made their livings as merchants or travelers. At a time when people depended on wind, water, and animals for power, ships were considered the most advanced technology. And ships from nearby and faraway ports constantly filled Venice's harbor.

Venice's powerful navy protected the city from repeated attacks by rival city-states. This allowed Venice's economy to thrive. To facilitate commerce, the city created an efficient business administration. Venice passed the first banking laws in Europe to regulate its banking industry. Venice adopted contracts spelling out obligations between merchants and shipowners. Beginning in 1253, insurance for such contracts became mandatory.

Historian John Julius Norwich wrote,

> A trading venture, even one that involved immense initial outlay, several years' duration, and considerable risk, could be arranged on the Rialto [in Venice] in a matter of hours. It might take the form of a simple partnership between two merchants, or that of a large corporation of the kind needed to finance a full-sized fleet or trans-Asiatic caravan . . . it would be founded on trust, and it would be inviolable.[2]

Venetians also formed trading partnerships with merchants of other lands, including Arabs, Jews, Turks, Greeks, and eventually the Mongols.

Venetian merchants traveled to distant lands in the Middle East, Africa, and other parts of Europe, either by caravan or by ship. They sought valuable gems, spices, and fabrics. Among the many items that merchants brought back to Venice were minerals, salt, wax, drugs, camphor, gum arabic, myrrh, sandalwood, cinnamon, nutmeg, grapes, figs, pomegranates, silk fabrics, hides, weapons, ivory wool, ostrich and parrot feathers, pearls, iron, copper, gold dust, gold bars, and silver bars.

The merchants also brought back Asian slaves. In the thirteenth century, slavery existed in Africa, Asia, and Europe, especially in the eastern Mediterranean. According to the fifteenth-century Spaniard Pero Tafur, slavery flourished in Venice. Tafur wrote that, "they say that there are 70,000 inhabitants [in Venice], but the strangers and

serving people, mostly slaves, are very numerous."[3] Indeed, Marco Polo owned a slave in the later part of his life. In his will, Marco stipulated that his only slave, Peter the Tartar, was to be freed upon his death. Marco also left Peter a substantial sum of money. Upon Marco's death, the Republic of Venice granted Peter the full rights of Venetian citizenship.

An amazing variety of goods continued to flow into Venice for hundreds of years. The great sixteenth-century English playwright William Shakespeare was well aware of Venice's reputation as a global center of trade and commerce. In his play *The Merchant of Venice*, Shakespeare has the character Antonio remark that "the trade and profit of the city/Consisteth of all nations."[4]

A powerful leader known as the doge ruled Venice. Each doge was elected sovereign-for-life by the Council of Venice, the city's council of oligarchs. The Venetian oligarchy consisted of 150 families that made up the city's merchant aristocracy. One of the doge's responsibilities was to protect the remains of Saint Mark's body. Saint Mark, Marco Polo's namesake, was the patron saint of Venice. In the year 828, a group of Venetian merchants had snatched the body of Saint Mark from its resting place in Alexandria, Egypt, and moved it to Venice. The body was placed in the doge's private chapel, where it remained.

The doge also represented Venice's mystical relationship with the sea. Each spring, on Ascension Day, a ceremony in Venice portrayed the symbolic marriage of the doge and the Adriatic Sea. In 1177, Pope Alexander III presented a ring to the doge, declaring, "Receive this as a pledge of the sovereignty that you and your successors shall have in perpetuity over the sea." The doge then hurled the ring into the sea, saying, "We wed thee, O Sea, in token of the true and perpetual dominion of the Most Serene Venetian Republic."[5]

In 1202, Pope Innocent III called upon Christians to join a Fourth Crusade to take Jerusalem from the Muslims. The Venetian Republic provided financing, ships, and supplies to the Crusaders. In April 1204, the Crusaders sacked the city of Constantinople (present-day Istanbul, Turkey) on their way to the Holy Land. Constantinople was the fabulously wealthy capital of the Byzantine or Eastern Roman Empire.

After the Crusaders moved on, Constantinople fell under the control of Venice. Much of the unfortunate city's finest statuary, precious gems, and religious artifacts ended up in Venice. Among the stolen treasures were four bronze horses that found a new home at Venice's Basilica di San Marco. Constantinople's finest artists, sculptors, glassblowers, silversmiths, and goldsmiths had to relocate to Venice.

The Basilica di San Marco in Venice. The four bronze horses on top of the Basilica were stolen from Constantinople by Crusaders.

⬤Education of a Young Venetian Merchant

Marco Polo was born into a family of Venetian merchants during the time of that city's rapid growth in commerce. The Polo family belonged to Venice's merchant aristocracy, although the Polos were not among the city's wealthiest nobles. However, Venetian records refer to young Marco as a *nobilis vir*, or nobleman.[6]

For the first fifteen years of his life, Marco did not know his father. Niccolò Polo and his brother Maffeo had left Venice for Constantinople and the East before Marco was born. At some point during his early childhood, Marco's mother died. So young Marco, raised by an aunt and uncle, grew up believing he was an orphan.

Marco most likely developed the urge to travel from his earliest years. Venice was literally built in the sea, rather than next to it. Most of the city's streets were actually canals.

As the son of a merchant family, Marco was destined to follow in his father's footsteps. He most likely received the education typical of sons of merchants. Instead of attending a grammar school where he would have learned Latin, Marco probably received vocational training. His studies would focus on practical arithmetic problem solving. This would prepare him for his future career as a merchant.

A present-day view of the canals in Venice. People still use the canals to move about the city.

This excerpt from the fourteenth-century *Zibaldone da Canal* (meaning "Miscellany" or "Ragbag") shows the type of problem-solving skills a young Venetian boy such as Marco would have had to master:

> Make me this calculation: 2 merchants have their wool on a ship. One of them put 13 sacks and the other of them put 17 sacks [on board]. And when they had arrived in Venice the captain demanded his freight charges from the merchants and they said to him, "Take one of our sacks from each of us and sell it and pay our freight costs and return the remainder." And the captain took 2 of these sacks and sold them and gave 10s. from the proceeds to him who had 13 sacks after the freight had been paid. And he returned 3s. to the man who had 17 sacks and his freight was entirely paid. And the merchants said to the captain, "We want to know how much you sold the sacks for, and how you calculated what you took from it for freight charges." [Follows the explanation of how the sum is done].[7]

The *Zibaldone* also included tips on business, taxes, and fees, and on how to set value on goods to be bought. There were notes in the book on converting foreign weights, measures, and money.

Most of the *Zibaldone* was devoted to preparing boys to become proficient in the various forms of mental arithmetic necessary to become a successful trader. How money was made and how it was counted took precedence over all else. But the

Zibaldone also contained material on astrology, weather prediction, and religious subjects, such as the Ten Commandments.

THE POLO BROTHERS: A FAMILY PARTNERSHIP

Niccolò and Maffeo Polo were united in a family partnership whose business was the buying and selling of goods. As merchants, their business required them to travel in search of goods to acquire and markets for their merchandise. Seeking wealth through trade in foreign lands, the Polo brothers departed Venice, probably sometime toward the end of 1253. They may have intended to be away from home for just a few years. But unforeseen events would prevent their return until the year 1269.

Niccolò and Maffeo Polo first sailed to Constantinople. There, they set up shop, trading with merchants from all over, especially those from the East. Business was so good that the Polos kept extending their stay. With each passing year, they grew more prosperous. But by 1260, winds of change began blowing through Constantinople. The city began slipping from Venetian control. Genoese, Greeks, Venetians, and others had taken to rioting in the streets. The Polos converted their money and other possessions to easily

transportable jewels. That year, the Polos left Constantinople and headed east.

Soldaia (in present-day Ukraine), a busy port on the Black Sea, was the next stop for the Polos. Niccolò and Maffeo's older brother, Marco, owned a house there. He had previously established a trading business there. For some reason, business

Niccolò and Maffeo Polo, at right on horseback, traveled to many cities and towns trading for valuable goods.

in Soldaia did not live up to the Polos' financial expectations.

Within a year, they moved on. The Polos wanted to return to Venice. But they decided such a trip was too dangerous at that time. Pirates had become active at sea, attacking any ships that crossed their paths. Meanwhile, marauding

bandits roamed the lands to the west of Soldaia. And in 1261, Byzantine (Greek) forces under Michael Palaeologus, allied with the Genoans, had seized control of Constantinople and restored Byzantine rule. Any Venetian traders caught in the city were imprisoned and tortured. The Polos certainly could not afford to risk passing through Constantinople. So they decided to travel east, where hopefully they could engage in profitable trade with the Mongols.

THE EMPIRE OF THE MONGOLS

For many centuries, the Mongols, an obscure nomadic people, had roamed the eastern steppe of Asia. The Mongol steppe, in the area of present-day Mongolia, was a vast, dry grassland. Around 1200, a local Mongol clan leader, or khan, named Temujin, rose to power in the Mongol steppe. Seeking to unite the clans under his rule, Temujin set about defeating his rivals.

By 1206, Temujin had succeeded in unifying the clans and took the title of Genghis Khan, ruler of the Mongol clans. Having accomplished his first major goal, Genghis Khan embarked on a path of pillage and conquest. The Mongol warriors were superb horsemen and expert archers. As the Mongol hordes swept across the steppe, they easily defeated all who rose up against them. A series of conquests resulted in Mongol control of all of

Central Asia by 1221. By the time of Genghis Khan's death in 1227, the Mongol conquest of northern China was well under way.

Ogadei, the son of Genghis Khan, became the Great Khan or ruler of the Mongol Empire after the death of his father. Under Ogadei's leadership, Mongol armies completed the conquest of northern China. The Mongols advanced westward as far as Poland. In the east, a Mongol army invaded Korea. In 1241, the Mongols had reached the eastern shores of the Adriatic Sea. They were poised to attack Venice and, farther north, the city of Vienna. But that year, Ogadei died. The Mongol commanders, and other sons and grandsons of Genghis Khan, were called back to the Mongol capital to elect Ogadei's successor.

The westward march of the Mongols came to an end with the death of Ogadei. In less than fifty years, the Mongols had conquered territory stretching from China to Poland. They had created an empire larger than the Roman Empire and the empire of Alexander the Great. The Mongol Empire was the largest unified land empire in the history of the world.

By 1260, the Mongol Empire was divided into four large khanates. Each khanate was ruled by a descendant of Genghis Khan. Kublai Khan, a grandson of Genghis Khan, named himself the Great Khan. He took control of the khanate

belonging to the Great Khan (present-day China and Mongolia). The other three khanates included the Khanate of Chaghadai (Central Asia), the Ilkhanate (Iran), and the Khanate of the Golden Horde (Russia).

⊕ THE POLO BROTHERS' TRAVELS IN THE EAST

Niccolò and Maffeo traveled on horseback, east across the steppe, along a northern branch of the Silk Road, an ancient trading route that linked China, Central Asia, Persia and western Asia, and Europe. Along their route, they encountered groups of nomadic Mongols living in round tents known as yurts. Finally they reached the court of Barka Khan in the region of the lower Volga River in present-day Russia. Barka, a grandson of Genghis, was the ruler of the Khanate of the Golden Horde.

Marco Polo wrote that Barka received the Polo brothers "with great honor and was very glad they had come. The two brothers gave him all the jewels they had brought; and Barka took them willingly and was exceedingly pleased with them, and gave them goods of fully twice the value in return. These he allowed them to sell in many places, and they were sold very profitably."[8]

The two merchants of Venice had found a safe haven in Barka's realm. They became accustomed to the lifestyle of their hosts. They drank koumiss, fermented mare's milk, and learned the Mongol language. In 1262, after spending a year with Barka, the Polos were ready to return home. But once again, obstacles arose. This time, a war broke out between Barka Khan and Hülegü, the Ilkhan of Persia, another of Genghis's grandsons.

Travel to the west was too dangerous. But the way east seemed safe. So the Polos traveled east, planning to come back later by a roundabout route. For seventeen days they journeyed across a desert. Eventually they reached the city of Bukhara (in present-day Uzbekistan), in the Khanate of Chaghadai. There, the Polos were hospitably received by Bukhara's ruler, Barak Khan.

Bukhara was one of the most attractive trading centers in the Mongol Empire. Niccolò and Maffeo established a thriving trading business in Bukhara. Though business occupied much of their time, the Polos kept looking for an opportunity to leave Bukhara. The Polo brothers were homesick for Venice. But warring tribes in the surrounding areas prevented safe travel.

One day, after three long years, an envoy from Hülegü Khan arrived in Bukhara. He was on his way to the East to visit Kublai Khan. When he met the Polo brothers, he persuaded them to accompany him on his eastward journey. He told them he could offer them an opportunity of great profit.

The envoy said, "Sirs, I assure you that the Great Khan of the Tartars [Mongols] has never seen any Latin and is exceedingly desirous to meet one. . . . I assure you that he will be very glad to see you and will treat you with great honor and great bounty. And you will be able to travel with me in safety . . ."[9]

In 1266, the Polo brothers reached the Mongol capital Khanbalik ("City of the Great Khan," the present-day city of Beijing, China). They were well received at the court of the Great Khan. Apparently Kublai Khan was very delighted to meet the Polos. He entertained his guests with magnificent feasts. Kublai was curious about the West and asked the Polos all about their part of the world. He wanted to know about Western rulers and their different methods of governing. The pope and the Roman Catholic Church especially interested him.

Kublai Khan was pleased with the information the Polos had given him. He was pleasantly surprised that the Venetian merchants could speak with him in his language. He decided to send the two brothers on their way home with a letter to Pope Clement IV. In his letter, Kublai Khan asked the pope to send him one hundred learned missionaries. He would assign these wise men to teach his people about Christianity and the seven arts of a medieval education—rhetoric, logic, grammar, arithmetic, astronomy, music, and geometry.

Kublai also requested that the Polos bring back to him some of the oil from the lamp that burned in the Church of the Holy Sepulchre (the tomb of Jesus) in Jerusalem. This "holy" oil was believed to heal all illnesses of body or mind.

The true reason for Kublai Khan's intense curiosity about Christianity is a mystery. Perhaps he considered converting his Chinese subjects to Christianity to facilitate his rule over them. Unlike his grandfather Genghis, Kublai was not a brutal conqueror. According to the Venetian historian Alvise Zorzi, Kublai was "a monarch pursuing high standards of governance, dedicated to learning and implementing the most efficient means to that end . . . he was constantly seeking better ways to govern and apply spiritual pressure points that would serve his aim of authority better than force."[10]

To guarantee the Polos safe passage along the thousands of miles of their journey, Kublai gave them "a tablet of gold engraved with the royal seal." This "golden passport," about the size of a man's hand, was called a *paiza*. It entitled its possessor to a supply of provisions, horses, escorts, and all other necessary help from local rulers throughout the vast Mongol Empire. The Polo brothers departed Kublai's court accompanied

Kublai Khan gives Niccolò and Maffeo Polo a "golden passport" to protect them on their return journey to Venice.

by Kogatal, the Khan's ambassador to the West. Kogatal became seriously ill during the first twenty days of travel and had to stay behind.

In April 1269, Niccolò and Maffeo arrived in the port of Acre (northern coast of present-day Israel). They had been on the road for almost three years. Their journey must have involved incredible hardships. They reported numerous delays due to heavy downpours, rampaging rivers, and deep winter snows. In Acre, the Polos met with Teobaldo Visconti, also known as Teobaldo of Piacenza. Teobaldo was the official emissary of the pope for the Church of Rome in the land of Egypt. He informed the Polos that Pope Clement IV had died in November the previous year.

The Polos told Teobaldo all about their amazing travels in the East and their meeting with the Great Khan. Teobaldo was happy to learn of Kublai Khan's interest in the Christian religion. He advised the Polos to wait for the election of a new pope before traveling back to visit Kublai Khan. So the Polos took passage on a ship bound for Venice. Upon their arrival, Niccolò Polo learned that his wife had died and that he had a son—fifteen-year-old Marco.

Chapter 3

Marco Polo's Journey to the East

The Polo brothers remained in Venice for two years. There had not been an election of a new pope. The two brothers were becoming impatient to return to the court of the Great Khan. They were afraid that if they waited too long, they would miss out on the chance of a lifetime—the opportunity to build a profitable trading business in the wealthy capital of the Mongol Empire.

Finally, in the summer of 1271, the Polo brothers set out on the long journey to once again visit the Great Khan in faraway Cathay. Niccolò brought his son Marco, a seventeen-year-old young man, along with them. For two years, Marco had listened to his father's stories about his travels in the exotic lands of the East. More than anything else, Marco wished that someday, he too could have such amazing adventures.

The Polos booked passage on a ship bound for Acre. Marco burst with excitement as they stepped aboard. Venice was the only world he had known for all of his life. Marco stood on deck as the ship sailed out of the harbor. He watched

Venice disappear in the distance. He had no idea that twenty-four years would pass before he would see his beloved Venice again.

THE POLOS AND THE POPE

When the Polos arrived in Acre, they met again with Teobaldo of Piacenza. He gave them permission to go to Jerusalem to get some oil from the Holy Sepulchre. The Polos traveled to Jerusalem, acquired the oil, and returned to Acre. According to Marco, the Polos said to Teobaldo, "Sir, since we see that there is no Pope, we wish to go back to the Great Khan, because we have delayed too long."[1]

Teobaldo gave the Polos a letter for the Great Khan. In it, Teobaldo explained that because a new pope had not yet been elected, the Polos could not carry out their mission. He also offered to inform Kublai Khan as soon as the next pope was elected. The Polos then set out on their long journey. When they reached the small bustling Mediterranean port of Layas, a rebellion broke out against the Great Khan. The Polos had to wait there until the volatile situation calmed down. While they waited, they received the welcome news that a new pope had finally been elected. And it was none other than Teobaldo, himself. He had decided to take the title of Pope Gregory X.

Pope Gregory ordered the Polos to return to Acre. This meant another delay in the Polos' journey. But they expected they would be rewarded for their troubles, and indeed they were. Pope Gregory could not assemble the one hundred missionaries that Kublai Khan had requested. However, he appointed two worthy wise men of the church to accompany the Polos on their journey, Brother Nicholas of Vicenza and Brother William of Tripoli. Pope Gregory gave them letters and gifts for the Great Khan.

The Polos set out from Acre once again, this time accompanied by the representatives of the church. They traveled on horseback. When they reached Layas, trouble was brewing again. The Polos heard about reports of brutal skirmishes in the area between Mongols and Muslims. The Mamelukes from Egypt were said to be attacking the lands that lay ahead of them.

Fearing for their safety, the two missionaries decided to turn back to Acre. But the Polos would not even consider such a course. After all, they carried with them Kublai Khan's golden passport, the paiza, as well as letters from the pope. Surely, they could expect safe passage through regions where hostilities occurred. Niccolò and Maffeo had already journeyed through these lands and lived to tell about it. So the Polos continued onward toward the distant lands beyond the eastern horizon.

By Land or by Sea?

As the Polos traveled east through Turkey, they saw Mount Ararat in the distance. Marco wondered whether he would be able to see Noah's Ark. The ark was said to rest somewhere atop the nearly 17,000-foot-high mountain. At first, he thought he caught a glimpse of Noah's Ark. But from closer up, he realized he had been mistaken. According to Marco, "this ark is seen from very far because the mountain on which it rests is very high, and there is snow there almost all the year, and in one part there is . . . a large black thing seen from far amidst those snows; but close by nothing of it is seen."[2]

Marco, his father, and his uncle crossed the arid lands of Turkey. As they traveled near the border of present-day Georgia, Marco reported seeing a geyser that gushed oil. He knew that oil was used to light lamps and as an ointment in treating rashes. Continuing southeastward, the Polos reached the city of Mosul (in present-day Iraq).

Marco roamed Mosul's busy bazaars and noted the variety of goods traded there. Although Marco enjoyed the excitement of the bazaars, the Polos did not stay long in the city on the Tigris River. The goal of their journey was far to the east.

Leaving Mosul, the Polos traveled northeast and crossed into Persia. They began traveling through desert. In each Muslim town they passed, Marco admired the graceful minarets that rose above the beautiful mosques.

Eventually the Polos arrived at Tabriz, an important trading center. The city impressed Marco with its thriving markets and merchants who traded there. In his book, he wrote:

> The people of Tabriz live by trade and industry; for cloth of gold and silk is woven here in great quantity and of great value. The city is so favorably situated that it is a market for merchandise from India and Baghdad, from Mosul and Hormuz, and from many other places; and many Latin merchants come here to buy the merchandise imported from foreign lands. It is also a market for precious stones, which are found here in great abundance. It is a city where good profits are made by traveling merchants.[3]

Upon leaving Tabriz, the Polos headed southeast toward the port of Hormuz on the Persian Gulf. They planned to seek passage on a ship bound for India. Eliminating a portion of their overland route, they hoped to reach the court of the Great Khan at an earlier date. Marco wrote about a town along their route called Kala Atashparastan, the Town of the Fire-worshippers. Marco believed that the people of that town actually worshipped fire.

The Polos passed through the town of Yazd, known for its fine silken fabric called yazdi. They then came to the Persian city of Kerman. Marco noted that the town specialized in the manufacture of equipment for mounted warriors—bridles, saddles, spurs, swords, bows, quivers, and various kinds of armor. The women of Kerman embroidered beautiful silk curtains. Just outside Kerman, Marco got a glimpse of the falcons for which the region was famous. Marco wrote, "In the mountains hereabouts are bred the best falcons in the world, and the swiftest in flight; they are red on the breast and under the tail between the thighs. And you may take my word that they fly at such incalculable speed that there is no bird that can escape from them by flight."[4]

Eventually, the Polos reached the great trading port of Hormuz, after a narrow escape from the Karaunas. The sea was a welcome sight after trekking many days across the Persian deserts. The Polos were delighted to see so many sailing vessels in the city's harbor. They expected it would be relatively easy to secure passage to India. But the Polos's joy quickly turned to disappointment upon a closer inspection of their selection of ships. According to Marco:

> Their ships are very bad, and many of them founder, because they are not fastened with iron nails but stitched together with thread made of

coconut husks. . . . The ships have one mast, one sail, and one rudder, and are not decked; when they have loaded them, they cover the cargo with skins, and on top of these they put the horses that they ship to India for sale. . . . This makes it very risky to sail in these ships. And you can take my word that many of them sink, because the Indian Ocean is very stormy.[5]

Niccolò and Maffeo were very experienced at calculating risk. Almost immediately, they realized that a sea voyage to India was out of the question. Unfortunately, they would have to take the slower and more difficult overland route. This meant backtracking as far as Kerman and then heading northeast across the high mountains and vast deserts of Central Asia.

ALONG THE SILK ROAD

The Polos traveled the 200 miles from Hormuz back to Kerman without incident. Apparently the Karaunas were busy marauding elsewhere at that time. In Kerman, they joined a caravan heading north to the desert oasis of Sapurgan. First they had to cross a sixty-mile stretch of salt desert whose poisonous green water was undrinkable. The Polos rode on Bactrian, two-humped camels, which could go for days without water.

The Polos followed the southern branch of the Silk Road. The Silk Road actually consisted of several main routes and many offshoots, one of which

The Polos arrive at the port of Hormuz on the Persian Gulf. Their journey to Kublai Khan's summer palace took them four years.

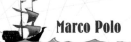
ran south, deep into India. The main northern and southern routes started in the cities of northern China. The different Silk Road routes developed because of the particular political history of various regions and certain obvious natural features of the landscape. The routes were being used as early as the second century B.C. Silk cloth from China was the most important and profitable product transported along the route. But many other products, such as porcelain, spices, gems, jades, and bronzes, were also carried.

Most traders along the Silk Road did not travel the entire length of the route. Rather, they traded all along the route, traveling in large camel caravans. At various oases, new caravans would be organized to transport goods to the next oasis. A camel trainer rode atop the first camel. Often a surefooted donkey would precede the lead camel, whose head was tied to the donkey's tail. This was considered to be the most efficient way to transport goods along the Silk Road.

Caravansaries run by local residents of the oases along the Silk Road provided a valuable service to the traveling caravans. The caravansary inn provided lodging and meals for the travelers. The caravan's camels, horses, and donkeys were kept in the large enclosed courtyard.

Journeys on the Silk Road were often very difficult and dangerous. Travelers had to endure extremely low temperatures and icy conditions on high mountain passes. They often suffered from frostbite and altitude sickness. In the deserts, travelers had to cope with heat and thirst. Sandstorms frequently sprang up without warning.

Poor road conditions also made travel difficult. The Silk Road actually consisted of an ancient network of irregular trails and tracks, rather than clearly marked and well-constructed roads. Winter snows and summer floods frequently obscured the trails, making them difficult to find or, at times, impassable.

Traders along the Silk Road encountered other obstacles. In various kingdoms and towns along the route, traders were required to pay customs duties. Local rulers often demanded additional payments in return for permitting caravans to pass through their territories.

Caravans loaded with valuable merchandise were always vulnerable to attack by bandits who roamed the deserts and steppes. Marco never mentioned whether the Polos carried any kind of weapons for protection. The Great Khan's golden passport and the letters from the pope probably helped them in some situations. But there must have been times when these items did not work. The Polos had to rely on cleverness to talk their way out of trouble.

With so many potential dangers, and so much uncertainty, why was anyone willing to assume the risks of trading along the Silk Road? The main reason was the opportunity for substantial profits. Wise merchants knew what they had to do in order to be successful. Trade goods had to be low in volume and high in value because there were a limited number of camels in each caravan to carry the goods. Merchants transported luxury items, such as silks, not bulky raw materials or essential goods for everyday use. Wealthy Europeans were willing to pay handsomely for silk and other products that were not produced in the West. So traders gambled on their ability to survive a journey on the Silk Road, overcoming its numerous obstacles and delivering the merchandise intact.

Across the High Mountains and Vast Deserts

From Sapurgan, the Polos traveled through the Persian mountains to the town of Tunocain. There, Marco was captivated by the beauty of the local Muslim women. Indeed, the young Venetian called them "the most beautiful in the world."[6]

Continuing their journey, the Polos entered Afghanistan. They traveled through peaceful valleys dotted with Muslim villages. Their caravan then arrived at the city of Balkh, much of which lay in ruins. In the year 1220, the city had been attacked by the Mongol warriors of Genghis Khan. As in so many other cities throughout Central Asia and beyond, the Mongols had slaughtered the entire population and practically leveled the once-prosperous city. Balkh never recovered.

Marco wrote that, "Balkh is a splendid city of great size. It used to be much greater and more splendid; but the Tartars [Mongols] and other invaders have sacked and ravaged it. For I can tell you that there used to be many fine palaces and mansions of marble, which are still to be seen, but shattered now and in ruins."[7] Marco was horrified at this vivid example of the cruelty of Genghis Khan. Years later, however, after becoming an admirer of Kublai Khan and the Mongol Empire, Marco would praise Genghis and describe him as a great humanitarian.

In the Afghan province of Talikan, the Polos spent some time trading. The area was rich in salt, almonds, pistachios, and corn. After making a profit, they moved on. When they reached Badakhshan, the Polos stopped to trade gems. The area was known for its fine rubies, sapphires, and lapis lazuli. Marco believed that the rulers of Badakhshan were descendants of Alexander the Great and the daughter of King Darius of Persia.

Marco admired the horses of the region and related a story about them. Apparently a long time ago, all horses in the region were "born with

a horn, with a mark, on the forehead like Bucephalus [Alexander's famous horse], because mares had conceived from that very horse."[8]

Marco, apparently a young man with an eye for the ladies, commented in his book on the typical fashion of the women of Badakhshan: "The ladies of the nobility and gentry wear trousers, such as I will describe to you. There are some ladies who in one pair of trousers or breeches put anything up to a hundred ells of cotton cloth, folded in pleats. This is to give the impression that they have plump hips, because their menfolk delight in plumpness."[9]

During his stay in Badakhshan, Marco became ill, possibly with tuberculosis. He was advised to go high up into the mountains. Marco wrote, "On the mountain tops the air is so pure and so salubrious that if a man living in the cities and houses built in the adjoining valleys falls sick of a fever, whether tertian, quartan, or hectic, he has only to go up into the mountains, and a few days rest will banish the malady and restore him to health. Messer Marco vouches for this from his own experience."[10]

The Polos stayed in Badakhshan for about one year. It may have taken that long for Marco to regain his health. The area was the leading producer of the opium poppy. Indeed, Afghanistan today is the world's leading opium producer.

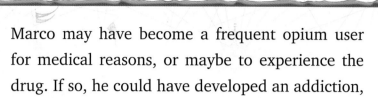

Marco may have become a frequent opium user for medical reasons, or maybe to experience the drug. If so, he could have developed an addiction, and it took time to kick the habit.

When Marco was ready to travel again, the Polos joined a caravan heading northeast along the Silk Road. With each passing day, they climbed higher and higher into the Pamir Mountains. The Polos began to suffer from the cold and the lack of sufficient oxygen in the thin air of the high elevations. The caravan ascended the Terak Pass and approached the farthest western border of China. They emerged onto a high plain on what is called the roof of the world. Marco called it the highest place in the world. At an elevation of 15,600 feet above sea level, they were surrounded by some of the highest mountains in the world, including Mount Everest.

Conditions were difficult on the high plain. According to Marco's writings, "This plain, whose name is Pamir, extends fully twelve days' journey. In all these twelve days there is no habitation or shelter, but travelers must take their provisions with them. No birds fly here because of the height and the cold. And I assure you that, because of this great cold, fire is not so bright here nor of the same color as elsewhere, and food does not cook well."[11]

Marco Polo traded for rubies, sapphires, and other gems in Badakhshan. This fourteenth-century illustration depicts Marco on horseback with ruby hunters.

After crossing the high plain, the Polos made their descent from the roof of the world. For forty days they followed the trail down steep mountain slopes and through deep mountain valleys. There, Marco reported seeing herds of wild bighorn sheep. These sheep have been named *Ovis Poli* in Marco Polo's honor.

Marco did not think highly of the local mountain dwellers. He wrote, "The inhabitants live very high up in the mountains. They are . . . utter savages, living entirely by the chase and dressed in the skins of beasts. They are out and out bad."[12]

The Polos were greatly relieved when they finally emerged from the mountains. In the towns of Kashgar, Yarkand, and Khotan, the local inhabitants provided supplies. Khotan was situated at the western edge of the Taklimakan Desert. In good spirits, the Polos headed east as they skirted the southern edge of the Taklimakan Desert. They eventually reached the city of Lop (Lop Nor in the present-day Xinjiang Uygur Autonomous Region in western China). Lop was situated between the Taklimakan Desert and the much greater Gobi Desert to the east. According to Marco, travelers were advised to rest at least a week at Lop before venturing into the desert. He reported that the Desert of Lop (Gobi Desert) was so long that it would take a year to travel from one end to the other. Even at its narrowest point, it would take a month to cross it. So the Polos rested at Lop and then packed enough supplies to last them at least a month.

As the Polos' caravan made its way across the desert, the brave Venetians endured great extremes of temperature. Under the burning

The Polos had to endure extreme conditions in order to cross the Gobi Desert. It took them one month to complete the trek across it.

midday sun, temperatures rose above 100°
Fahrenheit. At night, temperatures fell below
freezing. Despite the discomfort, the beauty of the
sand dunes captivated Marco. He gazed in awe at
the vast emptiness that stretched away to the horizon. But all along he kept watching for the evil
spirits who were said to dwell in the Gobi Desert.
Travelers were advised to stay close together and
not stray from the caravan.

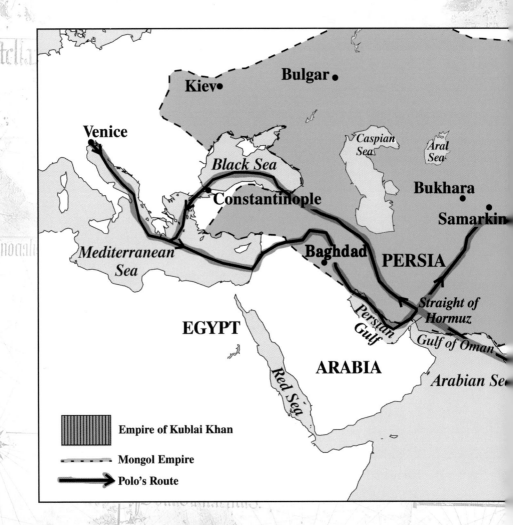

Marco wrote that when a man is riding alone through the desert, "he hears spirits talking in such a way that they seem to be his companions. Sometimes, indeed, they even hail him by name. Often these voices make him stray from the path, so that he never finds it again. And in this way many travelers have been lost and have perished."[13] Marco actually reported a very well-known phenomenon of the Gobi Desert called

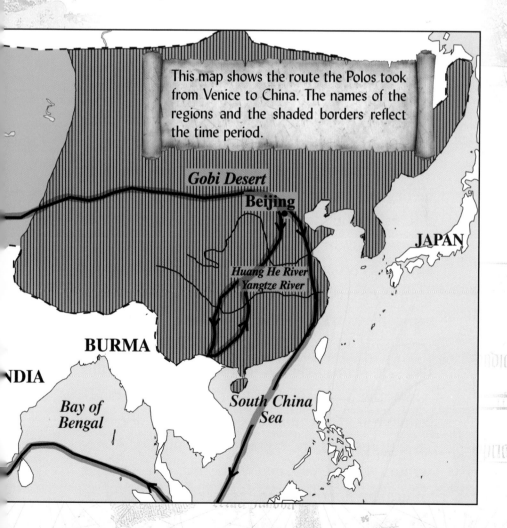

This map shows the route the Polos took from Venice to China. The names of the regions and the shaded borders reflect the time period.

Gobi Desert

Beijing

JAPAN

Huang He River
Yangtze River

BURMA

NDIA

Bay of
Bengal

South China
Sea

"singing sands" caused by the action of the wind on dunes.

The Polos finally emerged from the Gobi Desert into the western Chinese province of Tangut. There, Marco was fascinated by the animals known as yaks. He also wrote about the finest musk in the world, which was obtained from a gland of a tiny antelope of this region. Marco wrote about a local Mongol chief named Ung Khan, a Nestorian Christian who supposedly became the legendary Prester John. Prester (priest) John was said to have established a great empire somewhere in Asia.

As they stayed in one town after another along their route, Marco learned more about the beliefs of the "idolaters." The more he learned, the more he began to respect their Buddhist beliefs and traditions. At Buddhist monasteries, he appreciated the devotion of the monks. The religious festivals and feasts on particular days of the year reminded him of Christian observances. Marco even overcame his revulsion of the Buddhist practice of cremation because it showed him that Buddhists, like Christians, believed in a soul and an afterlife.

At the town of Kamul (present-day Hami), Marco was greatly impressed by the friendliness of its citizens and their gracious hospitality. Marco wrote: "I give you my word that if a stranger comes to a house here to seek hospitality he receives a very warm welcome. The host bids his wife do everything that the guest wishes. Then he leaves the house and goes about his business and stays away two or three days."[14]

After leaving Kamul, the Polos traveled across another desert. In the spring of 1275, the Polos were nearing the end of their long and arduous journey. When they were still about forty days' travel from the court of the Great Khan, horsemen from the royal court came to escort them the rest of the way. Finally, the Polos arrived at Xanadu, the summer palace and court of Kublai Khan. Xanadu (Shangdu) was located about 200 miles north of present-day Beijing. It had taken the Venetians almost four years to travel the 5,600 miles from Venice to Xanadu.

Chapter 4

In Service to the Great Khan

After their arrival at Xanadu, the Polos were taken to Kublai Khan's summer palace. They knelt before the Great Khan. Marco wrote:

> The Great Khan bade them rise and received them honorably and entertained them with good cheer. He asked many questions about their condition and how they had fared after their departure. The brothers assured him that they had indeed fared well, since they found him well and flourishing. Then they presented the privileges and letters which the Pope had sent, with which he was greatly pleased, and handed over the holy oil, which he received with joy and prized very highly.[1]

MARCO AND KUBLAI KHAN

Kublai Khan then pointed to Marco and asked the Polo brothers who he was. Niccolò replied, "Sir, he is my son and your man, whom as the dearest thing I had in this world I have brought with great peril and ado from such distant lands to present him to thee for thy servant."[2] Kublai Khan was pleased and said that Marco was welcome at his court. A great feast followed. The Polos were treated well, even better than all the other nobles at the court.

From then on, the well-being and personal safety of the Polos within the Great Khan's empire depended solely on Kublai's goodwill. They would have to do his bidding and carry out whatever tasks he might assign them. They would no longer have the option of coming or going as they pleased. They would never be able to return home without the Great Kahn's permission. Indeed, they would remain in Kublai's service for the next seventeen years. But Marco was thrilled to be in such magnificent surroundings and in such exalted company.

Marco had never before seen so lavish a palace. The enormous wealth apparent in its minute details and the ingenuity of the portable summer palace must have amazed the young Venetian. He wrote, "In this city Kublai Khan built a huge palace of marble and other ornamental stones. Its halls and chambers are all gilded, and the whole building is marvelously embellished and richly adorned."[3]

About five hundred years later, in 1797, the great English poet Samuel Taylor Coleridge would write his own poem about the amazing palace of Kublai Khan. Coleridge had been reading Marco Polo's description of Kublai's palace. He then fell asleep and dreamed about Xanadu. When he awoke, he wrote "Kubla Khan, or a Vision in a Dream. A Fragment." The poem begins with these famous words: "In Xanadu did Kubla Khan, a stately pleasure-dome decree."

At Xanadu, a 16-mile wall enclosed a private park, whose only entry was by way of the palace. Marco wrote:

> In the midst of this enclosed park, where there is a beautiful grove, the Great Khan has built another large palace, constructed entirely of canes, but

Niccolò Polo presents the pope's letter to Kublai Khan. Marco Polo would remain in the service of the Great Khan for the next seventeen years.

with the interior all gilt and decorated with beasts and birds of very skillful workmanship. It is reared on gilt and varnished pillars, on each of which stands a dragon, entwining the pillar with his tail and supporting the roof on his outstretched limbs. The roof is also made of canes, so well varnished that it is quite waterproof. . . . And the Great Khan has had it so designed that it can be moved whenever he fancies; for it is held in place by more than 200 cords of silk. . . . And he has had it so constructed that he can erect or dismantle it at pleasure.[4]

The Great Khan's summer palace and his royal lifestyle had a great effect on Marco. He noted that Kublai had a herd of more than ten thousand white horses and as great a number of white cows. Only the Great Khan and his descendants were allowed to drink the milk of these animals. Inside the palace, visitors had to wear special white boots so as not to soil the exquisite golden silk carpets.

At the end of the summer, Kublai dismantled his lavish, portable summer palace. The Great Khan and his court moved back to Khanbalik. The Polos accompanied Kublai to Khanbalik. The capital city of the Mongol Empire astounded Marco. Never had he seen a city of such vast dimensions and with such a huge population. Nor had he ever seen a city with such perfectly straight, wide

streets. The outer walls of the city, about 45 feet high, ran all along the 24-mile circumference.

The immense royal palace was situated within a walled inner city. According to Marco:

> The roof of the palace itself is very high. The walls of the halls and chambers inside are all covered with gold and silver and decorated with pictures of dragons and birds and horsemen and various breeds of beasts and battle scenes. The ceiling is similarly decorated—nothing but gold and pictures everywhere. The hall is so vast and so wide that a meal might well be served there for more than six thousand men.[5]

Within the palace grounds were separate buildings, each of which housed one of Kublai's four wives. Each wife was an empress, and each had her own court. Kublai held frequent banquets and feasts in the palace's great hall. Each year on September 28, Kublai Khan celebrated his birthday with the greatest and largest feast of the year. According to Marco, the Great Khan wore solid gold robes. At least twelve thousand nobles dressed in cloth of gold and silk were in attendance.

Not content to report merely realistic details of the Great Kahn's lifestyle, Marco sometimes resorted to fantasy. In this spirit, he wrote about Kublai's astrologers and their magical powers:

> When the Great Kahn sits at dinner or at supper in his chief hall, at his great table, which is more than eight cubits high, and the golden drinking cups are

on a table in the middle of the pavement on the other side of the hall ten paces away from the table and are full of wine and milk and other good drinks, then these wise charmers . . . do so much by their enchantments and by their arts that those full cups are lifted of themselves from the pavement where they were and go away by themselves alone through the air to be presented before the Great Khan, without anyone touching them.[6]

Marco swore that this happened. Indeed, according to him it was an everyday occurrence witnessed by as many as ten thousand people.

From his first moments in Kublai's palace, Marco was overwhelmed by the Great Khan. He felt honored to be treated with friendship and respect by the most powerful ruler in the world. The Mongol Empire included all of present-day China, Mongolia, Korea, Afghanistan, Iran, Turkestan, and Armenia, and parts of Myanmar, Vietnam, and Thailand.

As Marco spent more time at Kublai's court, his admiration for the Great Khan only grew. Marco wrote, "All the emperors of the world and all the kings both of Christians and Saracens [nomadic Arabs] also, if they were all together, would not have so much power, nor could they do so much as this Kublai Khan could do, who is lord of all the Tartars [Mongols] of this world."[7]

In the next few years, Marco came to truly appreciate not only Kublai's power and influence, but also the fact that he was a humane ruler. Kublai seemed to be very concerned with the welfare of his subjects. He distributed alms to the poor. When buying crops from farmers, he acquired far more than he needed for the royal court. He stored huge surplus quantities and distributed grain to victims of famine or drought or any others in need. Kublai also took steps to provide education for his subjects. He established a system of public schools throughout his empire.

Marco was so impressed with the Great Khan and his apparent enlightened rule over such a huge part of the world that he began to change his opinion of Kublai's grandfather, the ruthless Genghis Khan. Genghis had struck fear into the hearts of men all across Asia and deep into Europe. His Mongol armies had slaughtered entire populations of cities as they swept out of the Asian steppes on their murderous path of conquest. Yet Marco wrote:

> Genghis Khan was a man very upright: eloquent, and of great valor and of great wisdom and of great prowess. I tell you that when this man was chosen for king he ruled with such justice and moderation that he was loved by all and reverenced not as lord but almost as God, so that when his good fame spread through many lands, all the Tartars [Mongols] of the world who were scattered through those strange countries willingly held him with reverence and obedience for lord.[8]

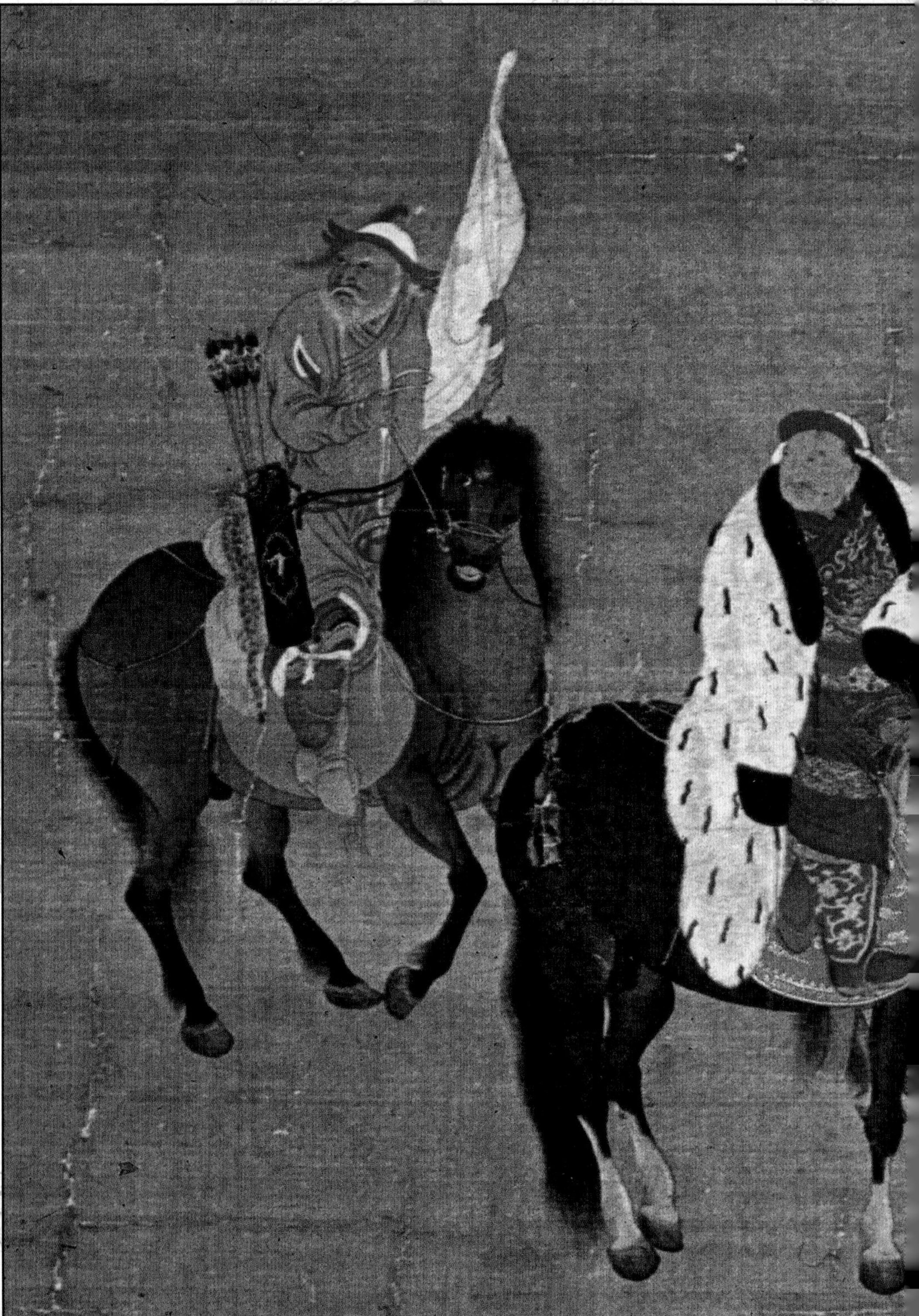

Marco Polo spent much of his time writing about Kublai Khan and his court. This painting on silk depicts the Great Khan's hunting party.

THE GREAT KHAN'S EMISSARY

Marco, Niccolò, and Maffeo were given fine apartments in the Great Khan's palace. When Kublai Khan saw that Marco was a gifted speaker, storyteller, and linguist who could speak several languages, he immediately took a liking to him. Kublai appreciated Marco's intelligence, curiosity, and enthusiasm. Kublai quickly realized that the young Venetian's qualities and abilities could be put to good use.

In his own words, Marco described his skills and attributes and why he proved so useful to the Great Kahn:

It happened that Marco, Messer Niccolò's son, acquired an impressive knowledge of the customs of the Tartars [Mongols], their dialects and their letters. It is a fact that before he had been very long at the Great Khan's Court he had mastered four languages with their methods of writing. He was unusually wise and intelligent and the Great Kahn was very well disposed to him because of the exceptional qualities that he saw in him. Noting his intelligence, the Khan sent him on an official visit to a country named Kara-jang, which it took him a good six months to reach. The young man fulfilled his mission excellently. He had noticed for himself more than once that when the messengers sent out by the Khan to various parts of the world returned to him and gave an account of their missions, they had very little else to say. Their master would then call them dolts and blockheads, saying that he would rather hear reports of these strange countries and their customs and usages than the official business on which he had sent them. When Marco went on his mission he was well aware of this, and he paid close attention to all the novelties and curiosities that came his way, so that he could describe them to the Great Khan. When he returned he presented himself to the Khan and started with a full account of the business on which he had been sent—he had accomplished it well. Then he went on to describe all the remarkable things he had seen on the journey, in such detail that the Khan and all those who heard him were amazed and said to each other: "If this young man lives to reach full manhood, he will certainly prove himself a man of sound judgment and worth."[9]

Kublai Khan sent Marco on one mission after another throughout the far-flung regions of his vast empire. Marco traveled to the city of Quinsai (present-day Hangzhou) to collect taxes. Upon leaving Khanbalik, Marco crossed a beautiful stone bridge that had been built in 1192. Today, the stone bridge, which crosses the Lugou River, is called the Marco Polo Bridge.

Marco traveled on horseback. Tall trees lined the sides of the roads. Kublai had ordered the trees to be planted to beautify his empire. Each night Marco stayed at a comfortable inn. The inns, called *yambs*, were spaced every twenty-five or thirty miles along the roads. Marco would soon discover that the yambs were an essential element of a highly efficient courier system throughout the empire. Fresh horses were kept in readiness for messengers at each yamb. Each village, at about every three miles between the yambs, also provided horses if need be. Riders galloping from station to station could go great distances in a short time.

Marco noticed that the inns were heated with black stones. The Chinese used coal to heat homes and to heat water for baths. Marco was fascinated by the black stones that burned like logs. Apparently, Marco had never seen coal in his native Venice. Coal, however, was being used at the time in a few places in Europe.

Along most of his journey to Quinsai, Marco followed the route of the ancient Grand Canal. Stretching over 1,000 miles from Khanbalik to Quinsai, the Grand Canal was the longest man-made waterway in China. The canal was a major route for shipping and commerce.

Marco was stunned by the beauty and grandeur of Quinsai. The city had been the capital of the Sung dynasty until surrendering to the Mongol armies in 1276. Marco estimated its population at about one and a half million, far larger than any European city of the time. Marco commented on the city's many canals, lakes, and hundreds of bridges. Quinsai's canal system reminded Marco of Venice. While taking care of official business, Marco also took the time to investigate the city's immense thriving markets.

Marco noticed that the people of Quinsai bathed daily in the city's hundreds of bathhouses. It did not take Marco long to realize why Quinsai was known as the "City of Heaven." Marco wrote that the locals used the cold-water baths, supposedly for their health. The hot-water baths were frequented by foreigners such as himself. About

Marco visited Quinsai, a large city in the Mongol empire. Like Venice, the city had canals, which are still used today.

the servant maids who worked in the hot-water baths, Marco wrote:

> These ladies are highly proficient and accomplished in the use of endearments and caresses, with words suited and adapted to every sort of person, so that foreigners who have once enjoyed them are overwhelmed, and so captivated by their sweetness and charm that they can never forget them. So it comes about that, when they return home, they say that they have been in Kinsai, that is to say in the city of Heaven, and can scarcely wait to go back there.[10]

Marco wrote that he returned many times to the City of Heaven.

During his long years in service to the Great Khan, Marco would travel to many parts of the Mongol Empire. Among the places Marco wrote about visiting was the province of Tibet. According to scholars, the region he described was actually Yunnan Province in southern China. Marco described hideous, monstrous snakes that could swallow a person in a single gulp. These monsters of the tropical rain forests of Yunnan were most likely crocodiles. Such creatures were unknown in Europe. In the mountains of Yunnan, Marco came across a hill tribe whose people covered all of their teeth with gold. In another tribe, the bodies of the men and women were completely covered with tattoos.

In Szechwan Province, Marco learned that salt was the main form of currency. The salt was cast in blocks, each imprinted with the Great Khan's stamp. Marco realized that the local inhabitants placed greater value on salt than on gold. He knew that traders could make huge profits by trading salt for gold. Indeed, Marco may have engaged in such trade.

Marco wrote about another form of currency used in Cathay—paper money issued by the Great Khan's government. Marco credited Kublai with introducing this type of currency. But paper money had actually been in use in Cathay for at least two centuries before the Mongol conquest. The idea that a piece of paper could be given monetary value simply by bearing the signatures and stamps of the Great Khan's treasury officials seemed amazing to Marco. To him, it seemed as if Kublai had mastered the art of alchemy, being able to change gold into paper money that was as good as gold.

Marco apparently did not realize that the paper money's value depended on the store of gold that backed it up. Nor did he understand that paper notes were an expression of credit—of Kublai's written promise to pay the amount described. Marco also did not appreciate the importance of the printing process in the creation

of paper currency. Printing, after all, would not appear in Europe until the fifteenth century.

In describing how paper money was made, Marco wrote:

> He [Kublai] has the bark stripped from mulberry trees . . . and takes from it that thin layer that lies between the coarser bark and the wood of the tree. This being steeped, and afterward pounded . . . until reduced to pulp, is made into paper, resembling that which is made from cotton. . . . He has it cut into pieces of different sizes, nearly square, but somewhat longer than they are wide. . . . To each note a number of officers . . . not only subscribe their names but also affix their seals . . . the principal officer, having dipped into vermilion the royal seal, stamps the piece of paper. . . . Counterfeiting it is punished as a capital offense.[11]

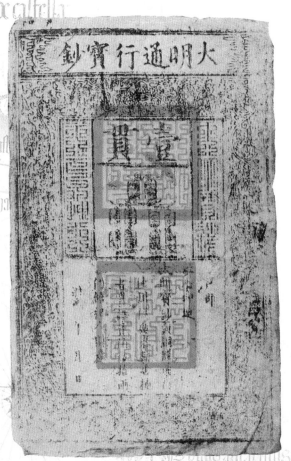

Kublai Khan used paper money as a form of currency. This bank note was first issued sometime between 1260 and 1287.

Marco's travels took him beyond the southern borders of Cathay into northern Mien (present-day Myanmar). Marco arrived there in 1278, one year after Kublai Khan gained control of the region. A desperate battle had taken place, during which the Mongol general Nescradin defeated the army of the king of Mien and Bengal. Marco gave a detailed account of the fierce fighting. He reported that the king of Mien's soldiers went into battle riding atop elephants. He described how the king's poor strategy led to his defeat.

When describing his travels through the dense jungles of Mien, Marco mentioned seeing lions and many other animals. Marco eventually reached the beautiful city of Pagan, with its spectacular golden and silver bell towers. Marco praised Kublai Khan for not ordering the magnificent towers to be taken down so that the gold and silver could be sent to Khanbalik.

During the seventeen years that Marco traveled as the Great Khan's emissary, he ventured far beyond Kublai's realm into India. He wrote about the Malabar and Coromandel coastal regions. Marco told how Indians of the Hindu faith showed reverence for oxen and refused to slaughter them. He also described how wives and servants of important men sacrificed themselves on their masters' funeral pyres. The pearl fisheries of southern India also interested Marco. He admired the skill and endurance of the divers who retrieved the oysters that contained the pearls.

Marco also visited Ceylon (present-day Sri Lanka), praising the island's rubies, sapphires, topazes, amethysts, garnets, and other precious gems. He traveled through Cambodia or southern Vietnam, which he called Champa. He may even have visited Zanzibar, which he wrote about. Marco also wrote about lands he did not visit, such as Russia, Korea, and Cipangu (present-day Japan). He described Kublai's failed attempt to conquer Cipangu.

At the end of each of his trips, Marco reported to Kublai all he had observed in great detail. Kublai was always gratified to be kept so well informed about the many peoples and cultures of his great empire and the lands beyond.

During the years that Marco traveled as the Great Khan's emissary, his father and uncle kept busy trading. They were pleased with the fortune in jewels and gold that they had accumulated. But as the years went by, they eventually grew home-sick. They were aware that the Great Khan was aging and his health declining. If Kublai died, they could be in a lot of trouble. Over the years, many of the nobles at court had grown jealous of the Polos' privileged position. Without the Great Khan to protect them, their lives could be in grave danger. Without Kublai's golden passport to ensure their safety, they might never be able to leave Cathay alive.

On many occasions, the Polos asked for Kublai Khan's permission to return home. But he always refused, considering the services of his Venetian guests too valuable to dispense with. Kublai enjoyed their company. And he had come to rely on Marco's informative reports.

Chapter 5

Return to Europe

By 1292, the Polos had spent about seventeen years in the service of the Great Khan. Finally that year, Kublai gave his permission for the Polos to return to Venice. But they would only be allowed to leave on condition that they escort the Mongol princess Kokachin on a sea voyage to Persia. She would be traveling there to marry King Argon, the Mongol ruler of Persia. Of course, the Polos were only too happy to agree.

The Polos and the Princess

It was probably just a matter of good timing that allowed the Polos to leave Cathay. When King Argon's wife Bolgana died, he sent three emissaries to Kublai asking the Great Khan to choose his next wife. Kublai chose seventeen-year-old Princess Kokachin to be Argon's wife. Kokachin left Kublai's court, accompanied by the three emissaries, named Oulatai, Apuska, and Coja. They planned an overland journey to Persia. After eight months of westward travel along the Silk Road, they entered a war zone in Central Asia. Fighting had broken out between rival Mongol tribes. The emissaries realized that the

princess's life would be endangered by continuing on through the region. So they turned around and traveled eastward until they arrived back at Kublai's court.

By lucky coincidence, Marco had just returned to Khanbalik from a successful sea voyage to India. Meanwhile, Argon's emissaries had concluded that a sea voyage through the Indian Ocean would be a much safer way to deliver Princess Kokachin to Persia. And they believed that Marco, because of his successful Indian Ocean voyage, could be of great help to them. So the Great Khan reluctantly allowed the Polos to join the group escorting Kokachin.

Kublai Khan entrusted the Polos with a new letter to the pope and letters to the kings of France, England, and Spain. He again gave them his golden passport, the paiza. And he probably gave them gifts of jewels. To ensure a safe voyage for the princess, Kublai had assembled a huge fleet. The ships thoroughly impressed Marco. The fourteen ships each had four masts and twelve sails—much larger than European ships. At least four or five of the ships carried crews of up to 250 seamen. The fleet carried six hundred people in addition to the crews. The Great Khan had provided enough provisions to last for at least two years at sea.

Marco described the Polos' departure from the Great Khan's court:

> When the ships were fitted out and furnished with food and with all things necessary, and the three barons and the lady and these three Latins, the two brothers Master Niccolò and Master Maffeo, and Master Marco, were ready to go to King Argon, they presented themselves to their lord, and took leave of the Great Khan and with great joy came to the ships that were prepared and assembled themselves on the ships with a very great company of ladies and gentlemen. And the Great Khan made men give them many rubies and other very fine jewels of great value, and also expenses for ten years.[1]

The Polos, the princess, and Argon's emissaries set sail from the southern port city of Zaiton (present-day Quanzhou in Fujian Province, China). The sea voyage would prove to be extremely hazardous and would take two years. They sailed through the South China Sea, the Indian Ocean, and the Persian Gulf. The voyage included a five-month stop on the island of Sumatra, which Marco referred to as Java.

Marco reported that during the course of the voyage, they saw many strange things and found many great marvels. But terrible things must have happened to the voyagers, because there were very few survivors. Marco wrote, "When they entered into the ships in the land of the Great Khan, there

People from Sumatra are gathering palm wine in this illustration. Marco Polo stayed on the island of Sumatra for five months while traveling back to Venice.

were between ladies and men six hundred people, without [counting] sailors. And when they reached the land where they were going, they made a count that all had died on the way except only eighteen. And of those three ambassadors there remained but one, who was named Coja; and of all the women and girls none died but one."[2]

If Marco is to be believed, almost all the members of the huge expedition met an awful fate. Marco does not give any details, but they may have encountered pirates or hostile natives. Some of the ships might have gone down in severe storms. Disease may have taken the lives of many others.

Marco wrote about a particular danger to ships along the coast of India. "This practice is followed throughout all these provinces of India. If any ship is driven by bad weather to put in at any place other than its proper destination, it is seized the moment it comes ashore and robbed of everything on board. For the inhabitants will say: 'You meant to go somewhere else; but my good luck and merit have brought you here, so that I should have all your possessions.'"[3] Marco did not indicate that this is what happened during his voyage. But perhaps this is indeed exactly what happened to one or more of the Great Khan's ships.

When the Polos arrived in Hormuz, they learned that King Argon had died. He may have been poisoned by an enemy. Argon's brother Quiacatu suggested that the Princess Kokachin marry Argon's son Prince Ghazan. The Polos escorted Kokachin to Argon's palace in northern Persia. There, Kokachin and Ghazan were married. The Polos prepared to begin the final leg of their journey home. But Princess Kokachin requested that they remain in Persia. She was afraid to be alone with strangers in a new land. Although they were eager to leave, the Polos had to obey Kokachin, since the wish of a princess was the law. Eventually, after pleading with Kokachin for nine months, the Polos received their freedom.

On the eve of the Polos' departure, a grateful Quiacatu showered them with fine gifts, including elaborate gold tablets or paizas. According to Marco, the tablets declared "that these three messengers should be honored and served through all his land as his own person, and that horses and all expenses and all escort should be given them in full through any dangerous places for themselves and the whole company."[4]

Princess Kokachin was very sad to see the Polos leave. Marco later wrote, "When these three messengers left her to return to their country, she wept for grief at their departure."[5] Sadly, Kokachin would die a short time later, in June 1296. She may have been poisoned by enemies of Kublai Khan.

This celadon pot is believed to be the only remaining object brought back from China by Marco Polo.

⬤ THE JOURNEY'S END

The Polos traveled overland by way of Tabriz to Trebizond (present-day Trabzon, Turkey), a port on the Black Sea. Somewhere along their journey, the Polos learned of the death of Kublai Khan. The Great Khan had died in his palace at Khanbalik on February 18, 1294. Marco must have greeted this news with profound sorrow. He knew that it would no longer be possible for him to travel in the Mongol Empire. Without the Great Khan's protection, such travel would be too difficult and dangerous. Never again would Marco set eyes upon Khanbalik, the Heavenly City of Quinsai, or any of the other magical places he had come to admire and love.

In Trebizond, the Polos ran out of luck. In this part of the world, their paizas no longer had the power to protect them. The local government of Trebizond confiscated a portion of their wealth. By this time, the Polos had traded some of their jewels for hyperpyra, gold Byzantine coins. Unfortunately, the Polos lost four thousand hyperpyra. The good news was that the Polos were able to depart Trebizond alive.

The Polos boarded a ship bound for Constantinople. Marco later wrote, "From Trebizond they came away to Constantinople, and from Constantinople they came away to Negrepont, and from

This is a hyperpyron, a Byzantine coin in use during the second half of the Middle Ages. The Polos traded some of their fortune in jewels for these gold coins.

Negrepont with many riches and a great company, thanking God who had delivered them from so great labors and infinite perils, they went into a ship and came safe at last to Venice; and this was in the year 1295 from the Incarnation of the Lord Christ."[6]

MARCO AND RUSTICHELLO OF PISA

Marco did not relate any details of the Polos' homecoming. But the three bold traders had probably long been given up for dead. After an absence of twenty-four years, the three Polos may have been unrecognizable at first. After the initial shock wore off, the Polos must have enjoyed a very warm welcome indeed.

Despite the money they had lost in Trebizond, the Polos still managed to reach Venice with a substantial fortune in jewels. Marco became one of Venice's richest merchants. In 1298, thanks to his high status in Venetian society, Marco received honorary command of a Venetian war galley. As fate would have it, Marco took command of the galley just as the bitter rivalry between Venice and Genoa turned to war. When the Venetians were defeated during the Battle of Curzola in September 1298, Marco was taken prisoner.

Marco spent a year in a Genoese prison. Luckily, his cell mate was a writer named Rustichello of

Marco Polo tells his story to Rustichello while in a Genoa prison. Rustichello turned Polo's stories into a book that was published throughout Europe.

Pisa. During his time in jail, Marco dictated stories of his travels to his fellow prisoner. Previously, Rustichello had written romances in French about King Arthur and the Knights of the Round Table. Now Marco's stories took hold of Rustichello's imagination and inspired him to put everything in writing.

If not for Rustichello, the rest of the world might never have heard of Marco Polo or his amazing travels. Rustichello's account of Marco Polo's travels would become one of the most popular books in medieval Europe. Written in French, it was soon translated into Latin, Italian, Venetian dialect, English, and other languages.

In 1300, Marco married a Venetian noblewoman named Donata Badoèr. The couple had three daughters, Fantina, Bellela, and Moreta. Marco remained in Venice for the rest of his life, where he managed a successful trading business until his death on January 9, 1324.

Chapter 6

The Impact of Marco Polo's Travels

The book recording Marco Polo's travels made a tremendous impact on Europe. It was recognized as the most important account of the world outside Europe available at the time. But many people were skeptical of Marco's account and believed it to be a work of fiction. They assumed Marco to be an experienced spinner of tall tales. Indeed, Marco's book was nicknamed *il Milione*, usually translated as Marco Millions. People teased Marco as a man who had a million stories to tell. It is said that when Marco was on his deathbed, his friends urged him to take back some of the most obvious exaggerations in his book. Marco supposedly murmured, "I never told the half of what I saw."[1]

MARCO'S BOOK

During his seventeen years in service to the Great Khan, Marco traveled to many parts of the Mongol Empire. He undoubtedly had all kinds of adventures. His writings about his travels describe in great detail the places he visited, the customs of the peoples, and the products of the various regions. Indeed, Marco's

Many skeptics believed Marco Polo's writings were fiction. But he said he "never told the half" of what he saw.

book was originally called *A Description of the World*. But unfortunately, Marco wrote very little about his personal experiences or thoughts. So a great deal is left to the imagination of the reader.

In those rare instances when Marco did relate his own experiences, it seems as if he exaggerated or even invented what happened. Marco reported that Kublai appointed him governor of the city of Yangzhou. He supposedly ruled the city for three years. This may or may not have been true. He was probably too young at the time to hold such a lofty title. There is no mention of his name as governor in any Chinese records. Of course, old records may have been destroyed.

Marco's book contained many inaccuracies. For example, Marco reported that he, his father, and his uncle took part in the Mongol siege of the Chinese city of Xianjiang. Marco wrote that his father and uncle designed and constructed siege engines, catapults that helped bring about the Mongol victory. Xianjiang was the last city in southern China to fall to the Mongols. But the siege took place in 1273, two years before the Polos arrived at Xanadu.

Marco's book was known to be a collaboration between himself and Rustichello. So scholars never determined exactly what Marco told Rustichello and what Rustichello may have added on his own. At least eighty-five early manuscripts of the book still exist. And each of them differs somewhat from the others. Yet scholars today regard Marco's book as essentially truthful. They believe it to be one of the most influential books of the Middle Ages.

MAPMAKERS AND EXPLORERS

Marco Polo was a great inspiration to future mapmakers and explorers. During his life, Marco received little recognition from the geographers of his time. But some of the information in his book was later incorporated into maps of the world of the later Middle Ages. Two important examples were the *Laurentian* (or *Medicean*) *Atlas* of 1351 and the *Catalan Atlas* of 1375. The *Catalan Atlas*, made by the Jewish cartographer Abraham Cresques for the king of Aragon, showed Central Asia and China very much as they were portrayed by Marco Polo. The *Catalan Atlas* included the city of Quinsai in Cathay and a picture of the Great Khan in his tent.

In the next century, Johannes Gutenberg introduced printing in Europe. Marco's book soon became one of the most popular books in print. It was read with great interest by explorers, such as Henry the Navigator of Portugal. Fra Mauro's world map of 1459 incorporated information from Marco's book.

A page from an early edition of *The Travels of Marco Polo*. This book helped inspire future mapmakers and explorers.

Marco Polo's description of Cathay and its riches inspired Christopher Columbus to try to reach the land by a western route, thus affecting the course of world history. A heavily annotated copy of Marco's book was among Columbus's belongings. Indeed, it was Marco's estimate of the huge extent of the Asian landmass that convinced Columbus that one could reach the East by sailing west. Columbus would make four transatlantic crossings in search of Asia, but he landed in the Americas instead. Marco's book played an important role in enabling Europeans to discover the New World.

For hundreds of years, Marco Polo's book remained Europe's primary source of information about Asia. Despite some elements of fantasy and exaggeration, the book contained an immense wealth of information about many different peoples, their ways of life, their religions, their histories, and the lands they inhabited. The development of the Renaissance that began in the Middle Ages in Europe owes much to Marco's revelations about the cultures of the East.

Marco was reported to have brought back eyeglasses in the form of ground lenses. These lenses would lead to the development of the telescope and the microscope. Galileo would use the telescope to support Copernicus's theory that Earth and the other planets revolved around the sun. Another Chinese invention Marco Polo described was gunpowder. Its introduction in Europe would revolutionize European methods of warfare.

In the epilogue of his book, Marco characterized his accomplishment: "But I believe it was God's will that we should return, so that men might know the things that are in the world, since, as we have said in the first chapter of this book, there was never man yet, Christian or Saracen, Tartar or Pagan, who explored so much of the world as Messer Marco, son of Messer Niccolò Polo, great and noble citizen of Venice."[2]

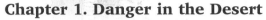

Chapter 1. Danger in the Desert

1. Marco Polo (translated by Ronald Latham), *The Travels* (New York: Penguin Books, 1958), p. 65.

2. Ibid.

3. Ibid., pp. 64–65.

4. Richard Humble, *Marco Polo* (New York: G. P. Putnam's Sons, 1974), p. 69.

5. Ibid.

6. Polo, p. 65.

7. Henry H. Hart, *Venetian Adventurer: Being an Account of the life and times and of the book of Messer Marco Polo* (New York: Bantam Books, Inc. [published by arrangement with Stanford University Press], 1942), p. 89.

Chapter 2. Two Merchants of Venice

1. John Larner, *Marco Polo and the Discovery of the World* (New Haven: Yale University Press, 1999), p. 36.

2. Laurence Bergreen, *Marco Polo: From Venice to Xanadu* (New York: Alfred A. Knopf, 2007), p. 14.

3. Henry H. Hart, *Venetian Adventurer: Being an Account of the life and times and of the book of Messer Marco Polo* (New York: Bantam Books, Inc. [published by arrangement with Stanford University Press], 1942), p. 16.

4. Bergreen, p. 15.

5. Ibid., p. 19.

6. Ibid., p. 25.

7. Larner, p. 37.

8. Marco Polo (translated by Ronald Latham), *The Travels* (New York: Penguin Books, 1958), p. 34.

9. Ibid., p. 35.

10. Bergreen, p. 27.

Chapter 3. Marco Polo's Journey to the East

1. Marco Polo (translated by Ronald Latham), *The Travels* (New York: Penguin Books, 1958), p. 38.

2. Laurence Bergreen, *Marco Polo: From Venice to Xanadu* (New York: Alfred A. Knopf, 2007), p. 45.

3. Polo, p. 57.

4. Ibid., p. 62.

5. Bergreen, pp. 51–52.

6. Ibid., p. 53.

7. Polo, p. 74.

8. Bergreen, p. 71.

9. Polo, p. 78.

10. Ibid., pp. 77–78.

11. Ibid., p. 80.

12. Ibid.

13. Ibid., p. 84.

14. Ibid., p. 88.

Chapter 4. In Service to the Great Khan

1. Marco Polo (translated by Ronald Latham), *The Travels* (New York: Penguin Books, 1958), p. 40.

2. Laurence Bergreen, *Marco Polo: From Venice to Xanadu* (New York: Alfred A. Knopf, 2007), p. 119.

3. Polo, p. 108.

4. Ibid., pp. 108–109.

5. Richard Humble, *Marco Polo* (New York: G. P. Putnam's Sons, 1974), p. 120.

6. Bergreen, p. 115.

7. Ibid., pp. 99–100.

8. Ibid., p. 92.

9. Humble, p. 142.

10. Ibid., p. 164.

11. Milton Rugoff, *Marco Polo's Adventures in China* (New York: American Heritage Publishing Co., Inc., 1964), p. 103.

Chapter 5. Return to Europe

1. Laurence Bergreen, *Marco Polo: From Venice to Xanadu* (New York: Alfred A. Knopf, 2007), p. 304.

2. Ibid., p. 305.

3. Richard Humble, *Marco Polo* (New York: G. P. Putnam's Sons, 1974), p. 194.

4. Bergreen, pp. 306–307.

5. Ibid., p. 306.

6. Ibid., p. 315.

Chapter 6. The Impact of Marco Polo's Travels

1. Richard Humble, *Marco Polo* (New York: G. P. Putnam's Sons, 1974), p. 209.

2. Marco Polo (translated by Ronald Latham), *The Travels* (New York: Penguin Books, 1958), pp. 344–345.

Glossary

banquet—A great feast.

Buddhist—Someone who follows the teachings of Buddha.

caravan—A group of traders or other travelers with their animals—camels, horses, and mules—journeying together for maximum safety.

caravansary—Rest stops at oases along the Silk Road that provided lodging and meals for travelers and care for their animals.

Crusade—Military expedition organized by the Christian powers of Europe to capture the Holy Land from the Muslims.

dialect—The form of a language spoken in a particular region or by a particular group of people.

doge—The ruler of the city-state of Venice.

emissaries—Agents.

empire—A group of countries that have the same ruler.

Great Khan—The title of the most senior Khan (ruler) in the Mongol Empire.

idolater—A person who worships idols.

khan—"Lord": a Mongol ruler.

khanate—A province of the Mongol Empire, ruled by a khan.

Mamelukes—Muslim warriors from Egypt who often raided the western Ilkhanate of Persia.

merchant—A person who trades with other people to make a profit.

Mien—Present-day Myanmar.

nomadic—Describes a member of a group or tribe who moves from place to place in search of food and water.

Saracen—Nomadic Muslim.

steppes—The arid plains of Central Asia.

vessel—A ship.

yak—An ox with long, shaggy hair.

yambs—Inns along the roads in Cathay.

yurts—Round tents of the Mongols.

Further Reading

BOOKS

Freedman, Russell. *The Adventures of Marco Polo.* New York: A. A. Levine Books, 2006.

McCarty, Nick. *Marco Polo: The Boy Who Traveled the Medieval World.* Washington, D.C.: National Geographic, 2006.

McNeese, Tim. *Marco Polo and the Realm of Kublai Khan.* Philadelphia: Chelsea House Publishers, 2006.

Otfinoski, Steven. *Marco Polo: To China and Back.* New York: Benchmark Books, 2003.

Senker, Cath. *Marco Polo's Travels on Asia's Silk Road.* Chicago: Heinemann Library, 2008.

Worth, Richard. *The Great Empire of China and Marco Polo in World History.* Berkeley Heights, N.J.: Enslow Publishers, Inc., 2003.

INTERNET ADDRESSES

Biography.com
<http://www.biography.com>
Search for "Marco Polo."

Marco Polo's Asia
<http://www.tk421.net/essays/polo.html>

Index